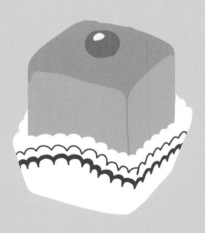

The
Art
of
Cake

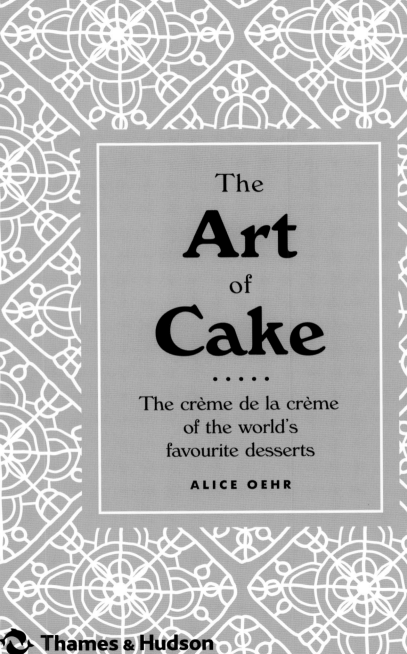

The

Art

of

Cake

· · · · ·

The crème de la crème
of the world's
favourite desserts

ALICE OEHR

Thames & Hudson

Contents

THE CAKES

HOMESPUN RECIPES

Introduction

Cake. The word alone is enough to stimulate
mind and appetite alike.

• • • • •

Admiring cakes, desiring cakes, remembering cakes past and dreaming of those we will go on to eat — even the simplest of cakes can inspire grandiose emotions.

My own love for cakes isn't founded in baking, nor even simply in their eating. Luscious flavours aside, it's the flamboyant decoration of the patisserie cabinet — each miniature creation a monument to pleasure — that never fails to lift my spirits. Where else in our lives do we see such flamboyant arrangements of colour, pattern and texture? Artfully placed berries, swirls of pastry cream, shards of chocolate and glistening jellies crown these little sculptures in shameless displays of fun. Behind the glass, they stand proud atop pedestals or on scalloped, gold-painted cardboard plates, inviting us to abandon reality for a moment and savour the delicious experience of having our cake and eating it too.

This is a book about the most beloved cakes from around the world, those made infamous across time and space for their triumphs of flavour, elegant simplicity, elaborate decoration and even for their brushes with celebrity and scandal. Here, we will meet cakes of both minor and major stature — from the basic no-bake cheesecake to the precariously towering croquembouche — and even some that are, *technically speaking*, pies or puddings. Every culture has their take on cake, and each creation is testament to the ingenious human ability to transform a few basic ingredients into something exquisite.

There's no question of the artistry of the professional patissier — painstaking puff pastry and nets of spun sugar are not for the faint-hearted — yet even the humblest of home-made cakes is a thing of beauty, a celebration of the time, effort and skill required to bring it to life. For many of us, the mere act of pulling a properly formed cake from the oven leaves us feeling accomplished (and probably a little relieved). Perhaps in honour of this, the sharing of a cake is one of the few remaining sacrosanct rituals in today's society — created for, and consumed on, significant occasions, cakes become embedded in our memories, laced with a heavy dose of nostalgia for the sweet moments of the past. It's this emotional connection that ensures our favourite cakes are unlikely to be the most expensive or the most artistic, but rather the slightly wonky, basic cakes made with love by a grandmother or friend.

While all cakes are things of beauty, I do reserve a special place in my heart for those that have been treated to a little embellishment — those with a maraschino cherry hat or a whipped cream cloak, replete with chocolate curls. Nigella Lawson demands a 'degree of vulgarity' when assembling her English trifle; and indeed, less is seldom more when it comes to decorating a cake — they're meant to be fun, after all. And though baking is certainly a creative endeavour, the true art of cake really lies in one's ability to enjoy it. Allowing ourselves a moment's pause to appreciate the good things in life is essential, especially where cake is concerned.

A Brief History

Though early cakes differ vastly from the
smörgåsbord of varieties we know today, humans
have always cultivated a sweet tooth.

• • • • •

Back in the BCE (Before Cake Era), basic breads were enriched with fresh cheese, honey, dried fruits and nuts and consumed at moments of ritual celebration. In those dark ages, to even be in the presence of a cake was a truly special experience.

Until fairly recently, the most basic of staple ingredients — fresh eggs, butter, refined sugar and wheat flour — were hard to come by, and luxuries such as chocolate, vanilla, spices, fruits and liquors were simply unavailable, by access or cost, to all but the top tiers of society. Even air — the one free ingredient required by all cakes — necessitates some culinary prowess to incorporate. Before food processors and chemical leaveners came to the baker's aid, a cake could only achieve the signature lightness that differentiates it from bread following hours of laborious whipping. And if you think baking is a labour of love now, in the days before widespread literacy even interpreting a recipe would have been an obstacle to many.

As time went on, cakes underwent various transformations at the hands of home bakers and patissiers alike. Chefs to the rich and royal evolved a genre of cakes all their own — only the tallest, most elaborately sculptured and outrageously decorated cakes would suffice for the decadent tastes of their audience — giving rise to truly audacious displays of gluttony. Some of these cakes existed merely as excessive demonstrations of wealth, with the flavours inside being secondary to their multi-storey exteriors of spun sugar, glacé fruits, flowers, ribbons and frosting. Indeed, one notorious early celebrity chef, Frenchman Marie-Antoine (Antonin) Carême (1784–1833), was famous among royalty for his architecturally inspired table pieces — lofty structures whose duty was to please the eyes first and palate second (if they were eaten at all).

In the 20th century, innovations such as the electric whisk, food processor and the gas (and eventually electric) oven meant that cakes became largely available to one and all. Packet cake mix was born to simplify the baking process which, together with the advent of cake decoration as a hobby for housewives, brought the focus back around to the look of a cake rather than its taste. Artistic arrangements of cream, jelly and fruits were once again in vogue.

Throughout history, cakes have represented the time in which they existed, ever evolving in appearance and contents to reflect fashions and available ingredients. Wartime, for example, has often inspired inventive substitutions of baking 'essentials' — molasses, fruits or vegetables sweetened cakes in place of sugar; chestnuts, rice or potatoes were ground up to replace precious wheat flour; vegetable oils stood in for butter; and powdered milk and eggs replaced their fresh alternatives.

Cakes are still the arena for much creativity today as bakers continue their experiments, creating confections free from animal products, sugar, wheat or nuts. Born of both practical necessity and the constant desire to innovate, cakes are always shapeshifting and updating their decoration. These days, we see slabs of cake, stacks of cake, rolls of cake and cups of cake decorated with icing, piped creams, fruits, nuts, jellies, flowers, sprinkles, edible photos and even gold leaf.

France deserves a special mention for its elaborate patisserie tradition — producing sweets that look and taste exquisite, and which require the sort of complicated techniques that only the bravest home baker might attempt. Other cultures are famous for their own culinary innovations, regional specialties, and particular styles of decoration. Most countries have their take on the basics — fruit cakes, cheesecakes, sponge cakes, chocolate cakes and ginger cakes, for example — that have evolved over time to include unique cultural twists that bring an exciting element of surprise to the otherwise familiar.

Cake recipes are steeped in tradition, with many people replicating the cakes they had baked for them in childhood. Modern cakes might be tweaked to reflect changing trends in nutrition and the tastes du jour, but the classics stand the test of time. Popular combinations tend to be almost universally agreed upon, regardless of time or place — coffee and chocolate, fresh cream and lemon, ginger and honey, alcohol and dried fruit and so on — making cake one of the greatest cultural levellers across the world.

The Cakes

Angel Food Cake

USA

Named for its heavenly texture, this extremely light
cake conjures up the sensation of eating a cloud.

• • • • •

The angel food cake is a pale version of the highly popular chiffon
cake, with one key difference: it contains absolutely no fat. Folklore
deems it light enough for angels to eat and still fly, unencumbered
by fullness. But, like qualifying for a place in heaven, baking the cake
is rather a delicate operation to pull off: a dozen egg whites are
thoroughly whipped with sugar, then flour is very slowly incorporated.
Subtle additions of vanilla or spices are optional, but strictly no egg
yolks are permitted, lest they weigh the cake down or colour it yellow.
The angel food cake is always baked in an ungreased tubular mould,
a combination of science and superstition behind its ascension as
it bakes. Often served with berries or a glaze, earthly beings have
been flying high with this cake since the 1870s.

In Southeast Asia, a vivid green version of chiffon cake is made using
pandan and coconut. In the Phillipines, a bright purple variation is
flavoured with *ube* (purple sweet potato).

Babka

EASTERN EUROPE/SLAVIC

A beloved yeasted cake that closely treads the
delicious line towards a bread.

• • • • •

Traditionally baked for Easter, in a tall, fluted bundt tin, the babka
(meaning 'grandma') takes its name from its supposed resemblance
to the pleated skirts of a grandmother — and, one could extrapolate,
from the feeling of comfort they reliably provide. A subject of
much reverence and many rituals, the babka is Slavic in origin, with
numerous incarnations having emerged from the many territories
where it is known and loved. The original babkas were plain, but the
addition of saffron, almonds, cheese or raisins has become common.
An Eastern European version is plaited with a delicious cinnamon or
chocolate filling, topped with streusel crumble and baked in a loaf tin.

In Poland, the babka would take a 'rest' on a feather duvet prior to
entering the oven. It would then be baked in a 'maternal' environment
that forbade men from entering the kitchen and any woman present
from speaking above a whisper.

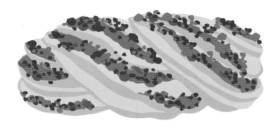

Baked Alaska

USA

Bringing an element of theatre to the table,
this showy dessert is a triumphant combination
of textures and temperatures.

• • • • •

Managing to be simultaneously hot and cold, the baked Alaska
was born in the late 1800s, when such complex desserts were all
the rage. Its main party trick is its miraculous ability to encase
frozen ice cream within hot meringue. This is achieved by topping
a sponge-cake base with ice cream (usually vanilla) and covering
the whole thing with raw, sticky meringue. Under the watchful eye
of the chef, the Alaska is then baked in a very hot oven until the
snowy peaks of the meringue are toasted. The secret of its success
is one of simple science: the air captured in the light sponge cake
and whipped meringue provides just enough insulation to keep the
ice cream cool during its brief time in the oven. Though certainly
a retro-style confection — having its heyday in the 1950s, and then a
revival in the 1970s — the appeal of a showpiece dessert is timeless,
and the baked Alaska still appears at special occasions today.

The *bombe Alaska* takes things one step further, by having
the whole edifice go up in flames at the table. One for the
pyromaniacs, this version sees the *bombe* (as such a spherical
or dome-shaped ice cream dessert is called) flambéed —
to wild applause — before serving.

Baklava

MIDDLE EAST, TURKEY, GREECE

A delicious diamond-shaped pastry stuffed with nuts
and dripping with syrup.

• • • • •

Baklava is one of those sweets whose success can be measured by the number of countries keen to claim it as their own. While it has many variations throughout the Middle East, baklava as we know it today was almost certainly developed during the time of the Ottoman Empire, at the Topkapi Palace in Istanbul. Classic baklava is made in a large tray, beginning with up to fifty sheets of paper-thin filo pastry, each brushed with butter. A thick layer of crushed nuts — almonds, walnuts, pistachios or hazelnuts — goes on, and a filo lid is added. After baking, the tray of baklava is drenched in a sugar (or honey) syrup flavoured with rose water, orange blossom water or lemon juice. Regional variations might be spiced with cinnamon and cloves, incorporate cream in the filling, or replace the syrup with a milk glaze, while Greek baklava is supposed to include exactly thirty-three sheets of filo pastry, to represent the years of Christ's life.

Needless to say, the assembly of baklava is something of an art. According to Ottoman legend, the layering of pastry and crushed nuts must be so delicate that a coin dropped on to it from a height would pierce each layer of pastry and fall right to the bottom of the baking tray.

Banoffee Pie

A 1970s love child of banana, toffee and coffee,
the banoffee (or banoffi, as it was originally spelt)
is ageing well.

• • • • •

This much-loved pie was developed by two chefs in East Sussex from an American coffee/toffee concoction they'd deemed less than satisfactory. Their creation employs a buttery pastry case to house layers of toffee, sliced banana and coffee-flavoured whipped cream. With a pleasingly retro flourish, the recipe insists that the toffee be made by boiling an unopened can of sweetened condensed milk for three and a half hours, until it turns into a thick caramel. Whether it was the perfect marriage of flavours or its catchy name that struck a chord, the pie became much imitated worldwide and brought fame to the Hungry Monk restaurant in which it was born.

The pie crust can be made with ginger snap biscuits to give the pie an added layer of flavour that couldn't possibly be incorporated into its name.

Battenberg Cake

UK

Any cake that can master a pattern has always proven popular, and certainly geometry is the most exciting feature of the Battenberg cake.

• • • • •

Two plain sponge cakes — one yellow, one pink — are baked and sliced lengthways, then glued together with apricot jam to form a square log. This is covered with a sheet of marzipan and, when sliced, the cake reveals its fancy chequerboard-patterned interior. This so-called 'domino cake' or 'church window cake' was proudly rechristened Battenberg cake in 1884, in honour of the marriage of Princess Victoria (Queen Victoria's granddaughter) to Prince Louis of Battenberg, and its colours were likely inspired by the marbled German cakes popular at the time of its invention. The cake remains a quintessentially British teatime treat.

The high-visibility chequerboard markings used on emergency vehicles in several European countries as well as in Australia and New Zealand are nicknamed 'Battenberg markings', after the cake.

Baumkuchen

GERMANY

The name *baumkuchen* ('tree cake') may serve merely
to mystify consumers – until it is theatrically sliced open
to reveal concentric rings, just like a tree.

• • • • •

The 'tree cake' is made by a labour-intensive process: using a pastry
brush, thin layers of cake batter are applied to a rotisserie spit. As
the spit rotates, the cake cooks very slowly (sort of like a kebab) and
as each layer is browned, another is applied, creating the distinctive
'tree' rings. Traditionally this would have been done on a stick over
an open fire — arguably an innovation of either the Germans or the
Hungarians, although many cultures stake a claim to some sort of cake
made on a spit. Once finished, the *baumkuchen* is removed and sliced
into tall cakes about 40 centimetres high, which may be served plain,
glazed with sugar icing, slathered with chocolate or garnished with
cream and fruit.

This cake is much adored in Japan, thanks to a German baker who
set up a *baumkuchen* shop in the 1900s and inspired many others to
follow suit. Today, crowds flock to observe the creation of the popular
spit cake through bakery windows, a display of skill and patience
that justifies the high price it commands.

Black Forest Gâteau

GERMANY

The allure of the black forest gâteau *(Schwarzwälder kirschtorte)* begins with its name: a romantic nod to the dark mystery of the German wilderness.

• • • • •

The actual gâteau reads rather deliciously too. Four layers of chocolate sponge cake are sprinkled with cherry liqueur and layered with sour cherries and whipped cream. The whole thing is entirely enrobed in another layer of whipped cream, covered with dark chocolate curls and decorated with a crown of cherries. In actual fact, it is named not for the landscape of its place of origin but for the local liquor made from sour cherries — *Schwarzwälder kirschwasser* — that gives it its heavy booze content. An alternative, more folkloric explanation is that its layers represent the traditional dress of the women of the Black Forest: white shirts (whipped cream), black dresses (dark chocolate) and straw hats, called *bollenhut*, with large red pom-poms on top (red cherries).

> The German name of black forest gâteau evokes the concept of *waldeinsamkeit* or 'forest loneliness'. This particular sensation overcomes a person when, alone in the wilderness and confronted with nothing but the vast expanse of nature, they are forced to contemplate the world around them, the particular quality of their existence and the meaning of life in general.

Boston Cream Pie

USA

In defiance of its name, this dessert is neither
a true pie nor a true native of Boston.

• • • • •

Strictly speaking, the Boston cream pie is actually a cake, comprising two layers of sponge filled with custard or pastry cream and iced with chocolate. This particular variation was developed by French chef Augustine François Anezin when he was working at the Parker House Hotel in Boston. The cake was brushed all over with rum syrup, its sides were spread with cream and flaked almonds and then, finally, the signature chocolate icing was added and decorated with swirls. Thus the Boston cream pie was born. Though none of these tweaks were truly original, the marketing strategy for the cake was rather cutting edge. In line with a post-war trend for changing the name of everyday dishes to include their region, this move transformed an otherwise unremarkable cake-pie into a classic piece of American history, irresistible to tourists and patriotic locals alike.

> Known as 'cream pies', 'custard cakes' or 'American pudding-cake pies', cakes like this were common across America in the 1800s. Baked in the same tins used for making pies, they fell under the same umbrella and so came to be called pies.

Bûche de Noël

A festive cake with a heavy dose of whimsy,
the *bûche de Noël* (or Yule log) is decorated like a tree,
with varying degrees of realism.

• • • • •

The cake itself is a simple tray-baked sponge, enhanced with vanilla,
coffee, chestnut, chocolate or rum. It is spread with buttercream
and rolled up into a log shape, often with extra bits added on to
serve as small branches, then the whole thing is coated in chocolate
ganache icing. Bakers with a flair for decoration can really shine
here — the chocolate outer layer might be combed into bark patterns,
and tree rings piped onto the ends of the cake. And when it comes to
accessories, the sky's the limit: meringue mushrooms, crushed-pistachio
moss, piped-icing spiderwebs, a sprinkling of sugar snow and green
leaves and red berries made from fondant icing.

The Yule log traces its ancestry to a real log, which was burned
around the time of the winter solstice to provide warmth and light at
festive occasions. This tradition faded, along with using fire as the
primary means of heating, but the cake version endures and exudes
a certain warm feeling all its own around Christmastime.

Cannoli

Hailing from the island of Sicily, these little ricotta-filled tubes achieve a wonderful balance of crisp shell and soft centre.

• • • • •

Cannoli take their name from the *canna*, or thick cane, around which thin circles of pastry were wrapped and then deep-fried to make the shell (modern-day bakers use steel tubes). The filling is made with sweetened fresh ricotta — traditionally the sheep's milk variety — and flavoured with candied peel, chocolate chips, liqueur or all of the above. To ensure the pastry remains crisp, the filling is ideally piped in just before serving, although a cheat's technique is to coat the inside of the shell with a thin layer of chocolate first. As a final touch, the cannoli may be rolled in chopped pistachios or decorated with candied cherries or peel. Originally cannoli were made in Palermo as a treat during the February carnival, but popularity has made them a permanent fixture across the country and beyond.

Varying in size from a tiny finger-sized *sigaretta* ('cigarette') to much larger versions, the cannoli is often co-opted as a measure of a man's physical prowess — which may or may not be connected to their history of being revered as a fertility symbol.

Carrot Cake

Carrot cake as we know it today is a dense,
textured confection that combines the grated vegetable
with walnuts, sultanas, light spice and a signature
cream-cheese icing.

• • • • •

While it may seem strange to modern-day Westerners with strong boundaries between sweet and savoury, the addition of vegetables to cakes has been widespread for a long time. Many culinary traditions combine meat or vegetables with what the Western palate considers 'sweet' ingredients, such as fruit, chocolate or vanilla. In times when sugar has been a scarce and expensive luxury, enterprising chefs have often employed vegetables that possess a natural sweetness in their desserts: parsnip, zucchini, swiss chard, pumpkin, beetroot, sweet potato and carrot all do the trick. Though this practice is less common today, the carrot cake remains very popular — and is, rightly or wrongly, perceived to be a healthy choice by virtue of its inclusion of a vegetable, brown sugar and (often) wholemeal flour.

> The humble carrot is the hero of many desserts around the world, perhaps most famously *gajar ka halwa*, which hails from the Indian subcontinent and combines cooked grated carrot with ghee, milk, sugar, almonds and pistachios.

Cassata

Not to be confused with an ice cream-based
confection of the same name, the classic Sicilian
cassata is a cake made with ricotta.

• • • • •

This lavishly decorated dessert is traditionally served at Easter, when
the sheep's milk ricotta is said to be at its best. Under a cloak of
marzipan lies a layer of sponge cake spiked with maraschino liqueur
or Marsala and a filling of sweetened ricotta dotted with citrus peel,
chocolate chips and nuts. The final cake-top embellishments vary from
pasticceria to *pasticceria*, but are always artful arrangements of glacé
cherries, silver balls, candied peel, candied pumpkin (zuccata) and
white icing piped into delicate lace-like patterns. More conservative
cassata cakes are enclosed in white marzipan but, as testament to
people's love for colour, the vibrant green version reigns supreme.

The *cassata* has gone out into the world and been reborn in
a couple of different ways. One version is made in the oven like
a traditional baked cheesecake, with a ricotta filling inside a pastry
crust. Its polar opposite is the *cassata* ice cream, which has layers
of different-flavoured ice creams — usually pistachio, vanilla and
chocolate — set into a loaf tin on a base of sponge cake.

Charlotte

Served hot or cold, the charlotte is classically
made in a tall mould, upended and decorated
in a manner that reflects her pretty name.

• • • • •

Charlottes come in two distinct versions, both with an outer lining of
crumbly cake or bread and a soft filling. A warm charlotte is built like
a pudding, using buttered slices of bread or brioche to line a mould
and make a casing, which is then filled with cooked fruit compote
— classically apples — before the whole thing is baked. The cold
alternative, a *charlotte russe*, is made with a shell of ladyfinger biscuits,
arranged attractively around the mould and enclosing a centre
of bavarian cream, chantilly cream, frangipane (almond cream),
chocolate mousse, fruit mousse or even ice cream.

The lady behind the cake is the subject of much speculation
and no concrete answers. Both France and Britain claim this particular
Charlotte as their own: the British say she was Queen Charlotte,
the wife of King George III of England. The French say she was
the wife of Tzar Alexander I, who inspired Antonin Carême to
create the *charlotte russe* in their honour. Another school of thought
entirely says the name is derived from an ancient English word,
charlyt, meaning 'dish of custard'.

◟ ◊ ◞

Cheesecake

For as long as people have been eating cheese, it seems
they have also been using it to make cakes.

• • • • •

Almost every culture has a cheesecake in its heritage, riffing on the
formula of soft cheese and sugar or honey, often with eggs to set the
mixture. Cheesecakes can be baked in an oven or chilled in the fridge,
with or without a crust, and flavoured with vanilla, spices, lemon,
rose water, chocolate, caramel, fruit or nuts. The earliest recorded
rendition of cheesecake comes from ancient Rome, and ever since
then people have been busy experimenting. In the UK, cheesecakes
are generally made with a buttery crushed-biscuit base, are set in
the fridge and often served with a fruit compote. In Russia, a crustless
baked cheesecake includes raisins and semolina; a special pyramid-
shaped Easter version, *pashka*, is flavoured with almonds, candied
fruit, vanilla and spices, and decorated with religious symbols. The
Japanese add matcha green tea and white chocolate to make a subtly
flavoured green cheesecake.

The famous New York cheesecake is characterised by the addition
of both cream and sour cream to give sweet and sour notes.
A 'twice-baked' version has an extra layer of sour cream added
to the top of the cooked cheesecake, before it is briefly
returned to the oven.

Croquembouche

VARIOUS

A spectacular and wildly elaborate tower of profiteroles
encased in spun sugar, named for the sensation
of consuming it: 'crunch in the mouth'.

• • • • •

The vast effort and expense of its creation means that the croquembouche is usually reserved for special occasions, such as weddings or christenings. As many as several hundred choux pastry profiteroles are baked and individually filled with whipped cream or pastry cream. Each one is then dipped in toffee and glued to its neighbour to form a tall cone shape. The whole construction is then draped in metres of spun-sugar threads known as *cheveux d'ange* ('angel hair'). Final flourishes such as almonds, silver balls or candied violets may be added to crown the cake.

> While today we mainly see the classic cone-shaped croquembouche,
> historically there have been all manner of grandiose incarnations –
> most notably at the hands of the father of French patisserie, Antonin
> Carême, whose studies in architecture influenced his creations in
> the kitchen. Carême's edible tabletop sculptures, or *pièces montées*,
> endeared him to royalty and the aristocracy in 19th-century France.

Dobos Torte

HUNGARY

Five storeys of sponge and chocolate buttercream
unite under a roof of hard caramel to make Hungary's
most iconic cake.

· · · · ·

Named not for the Hungarian word for drum (dob), as is commonly
believed, but for its inventor, József Dobos. Constantly tinkering in the
kitchen, like generations of his family before him, it was only natural
that this entrepreneurial individual would strike gold with his namesake
cake. The Dobos torta was unleashed upon the world — and, notably,
Budapest royalty — at the National General Exhibition of Budapest
in 1885. The cake soon became a sensation all across Europe, for
reasons beyond its flavour. Visually, the sheet of caramel on top of
the cake provided slick, minimalist relief from the overly tizzy cakes
that dominated the world of patisserie in those days. The chocolate
buttercream filling, too, was cutting-edge, and the subject of much
discussion — no one could work out the secret ingredient (which we
now know to be cocoa butter). Both of the aforementioned features
also helped to preserve the cake, enabling it to travel comfortably
beyond Hungary.

> In a final act of generosity and forward thinking, Dobos donated his
> official recipe to Hungary's Pastry and Honey-bread Makers' Guild
> so that all bakers might stop producing pale imitations of his beloved
> cake and make it as he intended.

Éclair

A baton of piped choux pastry, filled with cream
and topped with icing or toffee.

• • • • •

The éclair is named for the French word for 'flash of lightening', which should be all the time needed to scoff one down. Far simpler to create — and, as its name suggests, to consume — than some of the grander choux creations (think croquembouche), the basic éclair is a hollow tube of choux pastry filled with cream and topped with flavoured fondant icing or a glaze of hard toffee. The cream might simply be the sweetened vanilla cream known as chantilly, or it could be a pastry cream flavoured with chocolate or coffee. Contemporary interpretations see éclairs filled with pistachio and other flavoured pastry creams, caramel, fruit or chestnut purée.

Another popular take on the éclair is a delicate stack of two choux pastry puffs called *la religieuse*, after the plump nun in a habit it is supposed to portray.

Frankfurt Crown Cake

GERMANY

This German speciality invites us to imagine
a sparkling golden crown encrusted with rubies.

• • • • •

The artfully decorated *Frankfurter kranz* is an elaborate layer cake built of sponge, buttercream and jam, all without a cocktail sausage in sight. Three ring-shaped tiers of sponge cake are sandwiched together with buttercream and then slathered with more buttercream. The signature element of the cake is its coating of *krokant* — candied hazelnuts or almonds, which are deliciously crunchy and shine like gold. The final flourishes are added to the top of the cake in imitation of a crown: swirls of buttercream and maraschino cherry 'rubies' are the classic decoration. The crown cake was created to honour the German emperors' coronation ceremonies that historically took place in the city of Frankfurt, and it remains a stalwart in German cake shops today.

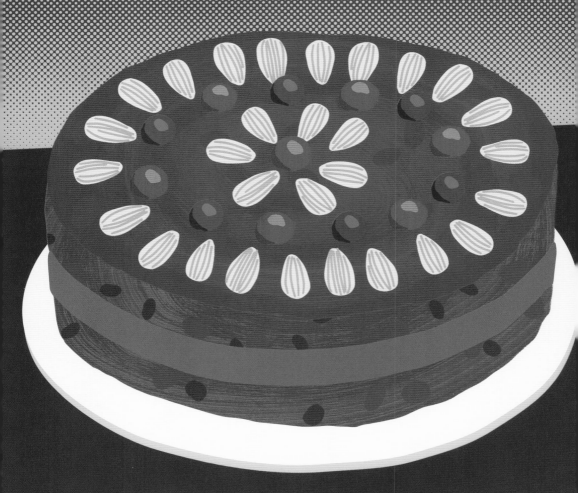

Fruit Cake

UK

The classic fruit cake is a sturdy combination
of very little cake and an awful lot of dried fruit,
all generously soused in alcohol.

• • • • •

Though most cultures lay claim to some sort of cake containing fruit, the most renowned version is British, with the fruit component normally comprising raisins, currants and mixed peel. Over several weeks or months, the cake is 'fed' with alcohol, usually brandy. Thus preserved, it can last for months — and often does, lurking in the back of the pantry. Celebratory fruit cakes come out at weddings, or Christmas, when they might be decorated with almonds, marzipan, piped royal icing, paper cut-outs, holly leaves and tiny model snowmen or robins. Early Roman predecessors to the fruit cake contained pomegranate seeds, pine nuts and raisins, but the export of dried fruit from warmer Mediterranean climes to Britain did not take place until the Middle Ages, and so we can date the British fruit cake's inception to somewhere around the 13th century. Its modern-day relatives include Italy's spicy panforte, Germany's stollen loaf and the Caribbean black cake, which contains even more alcohol (rum) than the British original.

The mysterious plum or figgy puddings referenced in Christmas carols and folklore are both versions of the fruit cake.

Gingerbread

VARIOUS

A confection that varies wildly across time and space, gingerbread is always spiced with ginger and mostly nothing like a bread.

• • • • •

Many cultures have put their spin on some sort of sweet treat containing ginger and other spices, such as cinnamon, cardamom, aniseed, cloves, nutmeg and pepper. Normally, the results are dark in colour and are sweetened with honey, sugar, golden syrup, treacle or molasses. Crisp biscuit-like gingerbreads are common across Europe and Scandinavia, many of them cut into little people, animals or other shapes and often stamped with designs, then either lightly glazed or elaborately decorated with icing. This same recipe is used to create the foundations for gingerbread houses, which vary in complexity from something like a dog kennel to a veritable sugar palace. Children are often recruited in the kitchen around Christmas to make them and, later, to help with the demolition. Other takes on the gingerbread biscuit contain nuts and chocolate (German *lebkuchen*), marzipan (Swiss *biber*) or fruit jam (Russian *pryaniki*). Both the UK and USA have a version of gingerbread that more closely resembles a bread: baked in a loaf tin, with the addition of oatmeal and treacle, it is often called gingerbread cake or simply ginger cake; the French version (*pain d'épices*) contains lots of spices and honey.

Scandinavian *pepperkrakor* are ironed flat then threaded onto ribbons and hung on trees and in windows, where they last for months.

Gugelhupf

A cake with a slightly confused Central European heritage and a multitude of spellings *(kugelbupf, guglbupf, gugelhopf* for starters), the *gugelhupf* is a culinary icon.

• • • • •

Born in the 1500s, and rumoured to be named after a hat or hood, the *gugelhupf* consists of a heavy, yeasted dough that is non-negotiably baked in a deep bundt tin. Raisins, lemon peel, slivered almonds, rose water or kirsch can be added to flavour the cake batter. It is traditionally served dusted with icing sugar, which settles into the cake's swirls like fresh snow. In medieval times, the *gugelhupf* would appear at weddings — adorned, like the bride, with flowers — and also decorated with fruit and candles. Marie Antoinette famously loved them, as did Emperor Franz Joseph of Austria, along with many thousands today.

The hat theory is a good one, but the cake is also rumoured to be named after the German word *kugel*, meaning 'round'.

Hummingbird Cake

Just like the exotic bird of its name, the hummingbird cake brings together a tropical assortment of banana, pineapple, spices and pecans under a lid of cream-cheese icing.

• • • • •

A Jamaican invention, the hummingbird cake was exported to the USA in the 1960s with hopes that it would find fans and entice them to visit the island. Before gaining worldwide fame, the cake was known locally as the 'doctor bird' cake, possibly due to the resemblance of bananas to the plumage of the red-billed streamertail hummingbird, or 'doctor bird'. Although, thankfully, it contains no birds, the cake is rumoured to attract nectar-eating hummingbirds with its sweetness. A luscious balance of textures is achieved with a combination of soft fruit, crunchy nuts and very little flour. Its substantial fruit content means that, even given the rare chance, the cake won't last too long.

Key Lime Pie

A native of Florida, this famous pie showcases its namesake citrus beneath a crown of luscious meringue.

• • • • •

Technically speaking, an authentically made pie must employ the juice of the Key lime, a smaller, sharper variety of the fruit that is especially tart and aromatic. A basic pastry case is filled with a mixture of lime juice, egg yolks and sweetened condensed milk — a favourite ingredient in the 1930s, when the pie was created. The whites from the eggs are beaten with sugar to make a meringue, which is generously slathered over the lime filling. In its early days, the 'icebox lime pie' was not cooked, as the ingredients would thicken and set on their own. Nowadays, it is considered risky to eat raw eggs and the pie is baked, with the added bonus being that the oven toasts the meringue.

> Some say the Key lime pie was created during long days spent out at sea by sponge fishermen in the Florida Keys. Not requiring any ingredients that couldn't be taken aboard a boat, nor any cooking, this may well be the only dessert invented while fishing.

King Cake

The king cake is known around the world – not so much for any sensational taste it may possess, but for the promise of finding the small trinket hidden inside.

• • • • •

Named for the three kings (or wise men) who came to honour the birth of Christ, this cake is traditionally eaten on January 6 for the religious feast of Epiphany, or Twelfth Night. The cake itself is usually quite plain, though naturally most countries have put their own spin on it. The French *galette des rois* differs across the country: in northern France, it is made from puff pastry, scored with patterns and filled with apple or frangipane (almond cream); in southern France — and Spain — a ring of brioche is decorated with candied fruit and sugar to resemble a crown. And in New Orleans, a purple, green and gold version has been adopted for the famous Mardi Gras celebrations. But the thing that unites all the variations is the *fève* (trinket) hidden inside, which represents the baby Jesus. The form the tiny prize takes can range from a broad bean to a plastic baby to a ceramic figurine, and all are much coveted by anyone eating a slice of the cake.

Various rights are bestowed upon the lucky person who bites into the trinket, hopefully with teeth intact — they might be named king or queen for the evening and must wear a paper crown, or, less luckily, they may be entrusted with purchasing the cake next year.

Lamington

AUSTRALIA

A modest concoction of plain sponge cake dipped
in chocolate and rolled in coconut, sometimes filled
with a layer of jam.

• • • • •

For such a small, unassuming cake, the lamington is surprisingly nice.
Born in Queensland in the late 1800s, the cake is supposedly named
after either the governor of the state, Lord Lamington, or his wife,
Lady Lamington. But, as with so many of the world's best-loved cakes,
the quintessentially Australian lamington was actually invented by a
Frenchman. In need of a dessert at short notice, the Lamington family's
French chef conjured up this simple confection using the leftover
sponge cake, chocolate and coconut he had on hand. Lamingtons
remain extremely well-loved today, and are frequently employed as
an attractive lure at fund-raising events known as Lamington Drives.

As with all cakes, the classic lamington has a number of variants,
each with their own fans. Some love a simple coating of jam beneath
the chocolate or in the middle of the lamington, while pink lamingtons
are dipped in unset jelly then rolled in coconut. Slice and add cream
for a decadent touch.

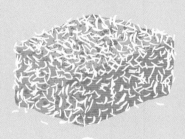

Lemon Tart

FRANCE

A much-appropriated French classic *(tarte au citron)* that in some parts of the world wears a meringue beret.

• • • • •

As its broad title would imply, the lemon tart appears in many forms around the globe, united primarily by the inclusion of the yellow-skinned citrus fruit. The French version employs a delicate, shallow pastry case to house a rich lemon filling made with eggs, sugar and lemon juice. Today, the lemon tart or tartlet remains a staple of France's patisseries, often simply decorated with a slice of glazed lemon or twist of lemon peel. Tradition also dictates a certain level of refinement in the French style of tart case. Baked correctly, the pastry is thinner and more delicate than Anglo-American pie casings, allowing the other few simple ingredients to shine.

> An English version of the tart appeared in the 1700s in a Quaker community and travelled to America toward the end of the century, where it evolved into Shaker lemon pie — a version that incorporates the whole lemon, peel and all. The lemon meringue pie, which uses the leftover egg whites from the lemon curd filling to make a meringue topping, was also developed Stateside.

Linzertorte

AUSTRIA

Containing almost every expensive and luxurious
ingredient imaginable at the time it was created,
the *Linzertorte* is a celebration of the sensual delights
afforded by great wealth.

• • • • •

Born in the city of Linz sometime in the 1600s, this evolution of the
basic almond cake is one of the world's oldest recorded recipes. In
its original form, the recipe called for prestigious ingredients that
were hard to get in those days, including almond meal, lemon zest,
fresh butter, eggs, cane sugar and white flour for the pastry, which
was lavishly criss-crossed over the top to form a lattice. In a truly
excessive demonstration of richness, the centre of the torte would
be filled with rare fruits like quince, peach or berries and spiced
with highly prized cinnamon, cloves, nutmeg and cardamom. Today's
version is most commonly made using a simplified hazelnut-meal or
walnut-meal pastry, cinnamon, cloves and redcurrant jam. The torte's
popularity endures, and it has spawned many offspring that marry its
signature flavours in tartlet or cookie form.

Until it was usurped by the invention of the *Sachertorte*,
the *Linzertorte* was the star of the Austrian cake world and was
counted among the city of Linz's main attractions.

Madeleine

FRANCE

A small buttery sponge cake made in the shape
of a scallop shell, the madeleine is a favourite
of French patisseries.

• • • • •

Though its enduring popularity is undoubtedly related to its pretty
shape, the madeleine is also a deliciously simple recipe that appeals
to all tastes: butter, sugar, eggs and flour are subtly flavoured with
lemon rind, orange flower water or brandy. Modern-day versions
all maintain the scallop shape, but experiment with fillings of jam or
lemon curd, a covering of chocolate icing or even the addition of
matcha green tea to the batter to colour it green. The cake originated
in the Lorraine region of France sometime in the 17th century; the
lady for whom it was named is the subject of many theories, none
of them substantiated. In the 1700s, the selling of the madeleine at
train stations fortuitously led to its distribution around the country,
where it won many hearts. To this day, just as Proust famously notes,
the madeleine evokes a powerful nostalgia for the simple tastes of
childhood and has become adored around the world.

In the 1800s, French chef Antonin Carême riffed on the
classic madeleine by adding currants, chopped pistachios, candied
peel or – most exciting of all – a coating of toasted meringue
to make a *madeleine en surprise*.

Merveilleux

BELGIUM

This small sandwich of meringues, whipped cream and chocolate shavings is named in French according to how it tastes: marvellous.

• • • • •

Originally born in Belgium, this cake was soon adopted by France, where it still appears in patisseries — and sometimes goes by the name of *boule au chocolat* (chocolate ball) or *boule de neige* (snowball). The cake's Belgian name recalls a group of rebellious female aristocrats in 18th-century Paris, the *Merveilleuses*. In the wake of the sombre massacres of the French Revolution, these women wore scandalously provocative clothing and revelled in luxury and decadence.

One modern-day French chef, Frédéric Vaucamps, has founded a whole patisserie empire devoted to the *merveilleux*. His versions, including praline, cherry and white chocolate flavours, have names inspired by the above-mentioned ladies: *magnifique* ('magnificent'), *excentrique* ('eccentric') and *incroyable* ('unbelievable').

Millefeuille

Hard to pronounce (unless you're French) and certainly hard to eat – at least delicately – the millefeuille is named for the 'thousand leaves' of puff pastry from which it is made.

· · · · ·

Traditionally, the milllefeuille is assembled in a stack comprising three storeys of puff pastry and two of pastry cream. To top it all off, it wears a hat of thick fondant icing feathered with chocolate. The cake's name is not merely romantic; it accurately reflects the fruits of the labour-intensive process required to make its pastry. For just one sheet of puff pastry, the chef must 'laminate' a dough of flour and water with butter, folding and rolling it repeatedly to create hundreds of paper-thin 'leaves'. After all the prescribed folding and rolling, a standard sheet of puff pastry should contain 729 leaves and, given that the cake consists of three layers, the millefeuille is, if anything, underselling itself. The cake is sometimes referred to as a Napoleon, due to a corruption of *Napolitain*, which describes the Italian tradition of creating desserts that contrast crispy and creamy textures. Unfortunately for the chefs of 19th-century Naples, the similarity of the word *Napolitain* to the name of the French emperor Napoleon Bonaparte meant that, along with all his work in Paris, this cake was claimed as just another of his triumphs.

As the millefeuille is really just a vanilla slice given the full-blown French patisserie treatment, most cultures have a less elaborate variation to call their own. These more basic, yet equally delicious, versions ditch the romantic name, along with the middle layer of pastry, and are normally built as a sandwich with a filling of custard, cream or both.

Opera

FRANCE

A beautiful marriage between coffee and
chocolate atop an almond sponge – eating an opera
might well inspire an aria.

• • • • •

Rather like a French alternative to the famous Italian tiramisu, the
opera is built on foundations of layered almond-meal sponge cake.
One side of each sponge layer is coated with hard chocolate, while
the other is soaked in coffee syrup. The cake is assembled with three
layers of this sponge, which are sandwiched together with coffee
buttercream and topped with a generous coating of shiny ganache.
A number of patisseries claim to be the inventors of the opera, with
its birth date varying more than fifty years between versions; the
Parisian Opera Garnier itself also lays claim to the cake, with the aim
of soaking it in lashings of coffee syrup being to help members of the
audience stay awake during lengthy performances.

Panettone

A refined, bread-like cake, the panettone is traditionally
served at Christmas with a glass of sweet wine.

• • • • •

The classic version is made from a rich yeasted dough of eggs, butter, sugar, candied peel and raisins. Its height and domed top are a feat of Italian architecture, recalling the cupola roofs of the country's numerous churches. Like all natives of Milan the panettone is elegant, sporting a special ruffled paper collar to keep it in shape and prevent it drying out. Its creation is an artform itself, as the dough must prove for several days if the cake is to develop its signature fluffy texture. Once cooked, it stands at least 15 centimetres tall and weighs more than a kilo. Modern takes on the panettone are (questionably) enhanced with the addition of chocolate chips, nuts and all manner of sweet centres like chocolate, pistachio, hazelnut or limoncello cream.

At Easter, the Italians have another opportunity to eat their beloved cake-bread as it reappears in the shape of a dove, as the *colomba pasquale*, sprinkled with almonds and pearl sugar. Festive season or not, the panettone and its fruit-free star-shaped cousin, the *pandoro*, are enjoyed dipped in morning coffees all across the globe.

Pavlova

NEW ZEALAND

Conceived and named for a Russian ballerina,
the pavlova has danced off the stage and onto the table
at many a barbecue or birthday.

• • • • •

Notoriously hard to perfect, this giant meringue is covered in whipped cream and, traditionally, seasonal fruit. While theoretically simple in nature, the pavlova is controversial in many areas. Subjects such as how soft one likes the centre relative to the crispness of the shell, or whether passionfruit is permissible, have sparked many an argument among families. A questionable retro variation for children's birthday parties calls for crumbled-up peppermint Aero chocolate bars, which stain the cream aquamarine. Toppings aside, perhaps the biggest scandal surrounding the pavlova is a cultural one. While it's claimed as the classic Australian dessert, the pavlova was in fact invented in New Zealand.

British food writer Nigella Lawson fearlessly added coffee to the meringue, slathered it with cream and a dusting of cocoa, and coined the 'cap pav' (cappuccino pavlova).

Portuguese Custard Tart

Though relatively plain-looking, to overlook these dainty,
bright yellow tarts would be a grave mistake.

• • • • •

The small flaky pastry cases of *pastéis de nata* hold a simple filling of
egg yolks, sugar, flour and a sprinkling of cinnamon, which is baked
until set and blistered on the surface. This is a recipe that showcases
the quality of the ingredients used, with little room for poor substitutes.
To meddle with the tarts' simplicity is to miss the point, though additions
of vanilla, cream and lemon are tolerated. Portugal's most famous
sweet treat was born of necessity, in a monastery in Lisbon during
the late 1600s. The monks went through lots of egg whites, which they
used to starch their robes and purify wine. So, they devised these tarts
to use up the leftover egg yolks and then sold them to raise money for
the upkeep of the monastery and their charitable works.

The *pastéis de nata* is beloved in all countries that have current
or former Portuguese populations, notably Japan and China.

Pound Cake

A rich, uncomplicated cake whose generosity extends
to providing a reminder of its recipe in its name.

• • • • •

In its most basic form, the pound cake calls for one pound each of
sugar, butter, flour and eggs. The French version is named *quatre quarts*
('four quarters'), on the assumption that one need only remember
which ingredients to use, and thereafter the recipe can be dispensed
with. Given that the cake dates back to the 1700s, when illiteracy was
commonplace, both names for the cake were especially helpful as
a reminder for bakers. Various flavours may be added to the basic
recipe to liven it up, such as brandy, vanilla, rose water or orange zest.
In Britain, glacé cherries are added to the mixture to make a cherry
cake, or madeira wine to make a madeira cake. In the USA, there are
many chocolate or marbled variations, and some partly replace the
vast quantities of butter with soured cream. In keeping with its humble
ingredients, the pound cake is traditionally baked in a plain loaf tin
and served only with a dusting of icing sugar. Slightly more festive
variations may appear in a bundt shape or with a light sugar glaze.

Prinsesstårta

SWEDEN

One doesn't immediately imagine the namesake
of a princess (or three) to be a vibrant lime green,
but this very delicate Swedish cake is just that –
with a little pink rose on top.

•   •   •   •   •

The *prinsesstårta* came to being in the 1930s, designed by a tutor to the
princesses Margaretha, Märtha and Astrid of Sweden. The girls fell
in love with the cake, which went on to have its very own Cinderella
moment when it discarded its rather unimaginative original title of
grön tårta ('green cake') to be rechristened the far more seductive
'princess cake'. Under a robe of pistachio-green marzipan sit three
layers of sponge cake, each spread with raspberry jam and vanilla
pastry cream. The final layer is topped with a huge mound of stiffly
whipped cream, which is responsible for creating the cake's pleasing
dome shape. As a final nod to its association with royalty, the cake
is dusted with icing sugar, drizzled with an elegant line of chocolate
and topped with a pink rose made from marzipan.

Considering the cake is not flavoured with mint or pistachio,
its green colouration has been a topic of much debate.
Was it the princesses' favourite colour? Does it represent the advent
of spring? Were the princesses' wedding flowers pink and green?
Many theories have been posited, but, alas, the true origin of
the shade remains a mystery.

Punschkrapfen

AUSTRIA

Beneath their thick pink icing, these small
but perfectly formed cubes conceal layers of rum-soaked
nougat, chocolate, apricot jam and cake crumbs.

• • • • •

The *punschkrapfen* is the Austrian version of a traditional 'punch cake', so named for its inclusion of a blend of the same spirits, fruit and spices — classically brandy, rum or arrack, citrus fruit and nutmeg — that flavour the popular celebratory beverage served from a bowl. It is unclear exactly when the *punschkrapfen* emerged, though it was likely in the 19th century, in keeping with the fashion for French *petit fours*: cakes made in miniature for both convenience and the luxurious possibility of sampling a generous selection on festive occasions. They are generally adorned with a drizzle of chocolate icing and a glacé cherry, and they remain very popular across the country today.

Cakes flavoured with punch appear throughout Eastern Europe
and Scandinavia: all boozy, each slightly different. In Sweden,
punschrullar are made with alcohol-soaked biscuits and chocolate
and enveloped in green marzipan. In Germany, Austria and Hungary,
the *punschtorte* is a rum and citrus confection; and in Finland,
the *Runeberg torte* is a pastry made with almonds, punsch liqueur
and raspberry jam.

Red Velvet Cake

USA

With its deliciously seductive name, the red velvet cake
is really just a chocolate cake that has been elevated
to regal status by red pigment.

• • • • •

At its inception, the cake used an untreated cocoa powder that
simply appears more red than the Dutch-processed variety that has
since become the norm. Today, its hallmark crimson shade comes
from the inclusion of either beetroot juice (a wartime practice) or
the ultimate fear-inducing substance for parents with young children:
red food colouring. The cake is normally stacked in two or more
layers and spread with luscious cream cheese or ermine icing, which
provides a striking contrast to the deep red cake. Not even the highly
unappetising armadillo-shaped red velvet cake in the 1980s film *Steel
Magnolias* could put people off, and it retains its popularity today —
in towering layered versions and oversized cupcakes alike.

Back in the 1800s, cocoa was added to flour in cakes to obtain a
smoother and more luxurious texture. This was a raging success,
spawning not only the red velvet cake, but also the mahogany cake
and the devil's food cake, among others.

Rum Baba

FRANCE

The boozy little French cousin of the panettone,
babka and *gugelhupf*.

• • • • •

One story goes that the baba was first imbued with alcohol as
a practical means of rescuing a dried-up old *gugelhupf*. It's said that
Stanislaus I, the exiled king of Poland, had one of his chefs douse
the cake with sweet wine and garnish it with fresh raisins and pastry
cream. This proved to be a very popular solution, as modern versions
of the baba all include the alcohol, the cream and often the raisins
too. Rum, or rum essence, has become the preferred soaking solution,
and the dry, bread-like composition of the baba cake makes it well
suited to soaking it up. Current-day babas are usually made in single-
serve portions, either in a small ring (like a doughnut) or a cylindrical
shape with a head (like a mushroom). The cakes are best left to dry
out a bit before being bathed in alcohol and garnished with whipped
cream. At fancy restaurants the rum may even be flamboyantly poured
over the baba at the table and set on fire.

> Talking of fire, the citizens of Naples have staked their own claim
> to the rum baba, adopting it as a classic Neapolitan dish. In the
> ultimate display of dedication, there exists the *baba Vesuvio*, a giant
> version of the cake in the shape of the local volcano, Mount Vesuvius.

Sachertorte

AUSTRIA

A luscious chocolate sponge cake characterised
by apricot jam and a scandal.

• • • • •

Created in the 1800s by chef Franz Sacher, at the command of Prince
Klemens von Metternich, the *Sachertorte* was later named as such by
Eduard, the chef's son. Contention arose between two parties who
both laid claim to be serving the 'original' *Sachertorte* in their institution,
and the exact placement of the apricot jam within the cake was also a
matter of hot debate. Demel Pastry Shop would glaze the top of their
cake with apricot jam before adding the chocolate icing, whereas
Hotel Sacher would split the chocolate sponge in half and spread
the jam in the centre of the cake. Hotel Sacher won the court case
that ensued and, to this day, still serve the 'genuine *Sachertorte*', with
its layer of thick chocolate icing and 'Sacher' inscribed in chocolate
on the top. Consumers don't let the 'torte wars' interfere with their
love for the cake, though, as they continue to enjoy it at Vienna's many
famous coffee houses and much further afield.

Smörgåstårta

SWEDEN

This highly decorated Swedish favourite is the
surprising marriage between a layer cake
and a lunchtime sandwich.

• • • • •

Adorned with smoked salmon, capers, caviar, prawns, olives, sliced
cucumber, dill, tomatoes and all manner of other herbs and vegetables,
the *smörgåstårta* translates literally as 'sandwich cake'. Under the
decoration, the cake is built from the unlikely combination of sliced
white or rye bread and savoury fillings, all glued together with
mayonnaise and slathered with cream cheese. It nearly always starts
with a base of hard-boiled eggs and mayonnaise and then ascends,
like a regular layer cake, in storeys of bread and various sandwich
fillings. These vary greatly, but might include liver pâté, ham, salmon,
tuna, pesto and cheese. Taking into consideration the fact that it is
very large, complex to construct and rather rich, the *smörgåstårta*
appears at special occasions rather than as day-to-day lunch fodder.
It is sliced up like a regular layer cake and served cold.

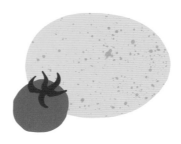

Sponge Cake

Named for its resemblance to the sea creature with much
the same texture, this light, airy cake appears in myriad
varieties and flavours in almost every culture.

• • • • •

Correctly made, the sponge cake says more about the technical
prowess of the baker than the simple ingredients from which it is
created. Flour, sugar, butter and eggs are leavened with the magical
ingredient of air, incorporated through prolonged whipping by the
increasingly tired arms of the chef. Sometimes, a little baking powder
is added to help the cake achieve the desired height. Consumed plain,
or with minimal decoration, the cake makes a deliciously light treat.
The British Victoria sponge is a classic: named for the queen who
enjoyed it for afternoon tea, this simple version has the sponge cut
in two and layered with berry jam and cream. By virtue of its airy, dry
texture, the sponge also lends itself to many other desserts as it's the
perfect vehicle for soaking up creams and juices. It is the sponge, in
its various iterations, that provides structural support for most of the
world's favourite puddings, whether rolled, stacked or cut into fingers
and decoratively arranged around any number of creams, sauces,
mousses, fruits or other fillings.

**The sponge has an almost infinite number of siblings around the world
— notably the genoise in Italy and the chiffon cake in America.**

Strawberry Shortcake

UK

A dainty little cake that takes full advantage
of the good looks of the strawberry.

• • • • •

Born in Britain and beloved in America, the strawberry shortcake has
notably risen to superstardom in Japan, where it has become an icon of
convenience-store confectionery. Originally, the cake was assembled
as a sandwich of buttery shortbread biscuits, with macerated
strawberries and vanilla-flavoured whipped cream in the centre and
as decoration on top. The cakes were made in biscuit-sized portions —
and always during the summer strawberry season as a celebration of
the fruit. The Japanese version was conceived when the enterprising
Mr Fujii visited America in the early 1900s and created his twist on
a cake he sampled there. He substituted sponge cake for the harder
shortbread base, and displayed sliced strawberries attractively in a
ring around the centre of the cake. This new version was so popular
that it provided the foundation for a whole confectionery company.

In current-day Japan, perfectly rectangular slabs of strawberry
shortcake are a classic choice for Christmas Day, along with
Kentucky Fried Chicken.

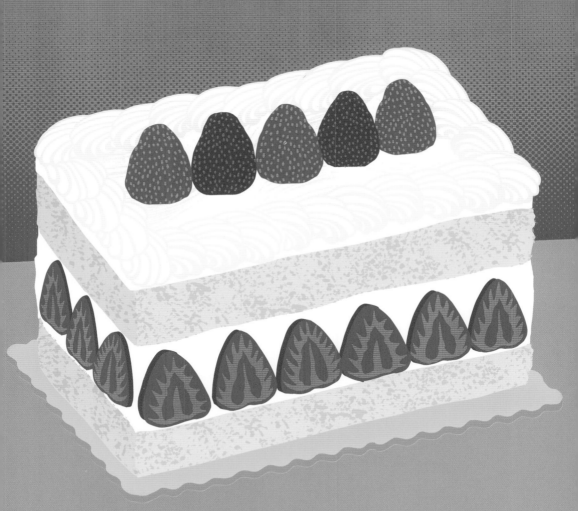

Swiss Roll

This rolled-up treatment of the sponge cake wins more points for design and creativity than it does for flavour.

• • • • •

A large, but thin, slab of sponge cake is baked, spread with jam or flavoured cream and then rolled up and sliced open to reveal its inner swirl. This relatively plain cake survives as testament to people's love of simple things and an attractive design. Though it is not Swiss — having most likely originated in Austria — this detail has been cheerfully overlooked by consumers around the world, who continue to love it whether they know it as swiss roll, jam roll or roulade. In the UK, the jam roll is a plain cake rolled with red jam and dusted with sugar. It is the sort of bland, dry cake that just begs to be dipped in tea, or soaked in brandy and custard — as is commonly done when it is used in a trifle. The French word 'roulade' is used throughout Europe for versions of the cake that are rolled up with chocolate, cream or fruit compote and usually served with coffee. In the USA, there exists a frozen version of the swiss roll that layers sponge with ice cream.

Tiramisu

ITALY

Arguably Italy's most famous dessert, after gelato, tiramisu offers the promise of a pick-me-up, and perhaps even an aphrodisiac.

· · · · ·

This is a dish that inspires many impassioned conversations about its method of preparation, but certain ingredients are universally agreed upon. Italian Savoiardi (ladyfinger) biscuits are soaked in coffee, dusted with cocoa and assembled in layers with a rich cream of mascarpone, eggs and sugar. Marsala wine can be added as it is, or first beaten with sugar and egg yolks into a luscious foamy custard called *zabaglione*. Personal preference determines the various notes of flavour and texture that shine through the dessert. It can be a light and sweet mocha affair, or a darker, bittersweet version, steeped in coffee and booze. In form, it can vary from a fairly sloppy pudding to a stiffly formed cake. Tiramisu is believed to have emerged from a restaurant in Treviso in the 1960s, though naturally there is much debate around exactly who made it first. And, like all good recipes, it likely evolved from an earlier version of something similar.

Tres Leches Cake

MEXICO

Do not be fooled by the innocent appearance
of the tres leches cake, there is far more to this little
señorita than meets the eye.

• • • • •

Baked in a large tray, a simple sponge cake makes the perfect
vehicle for the three forms of dairy for which the dessert is named:
evaporated milk, condensed milk and a luscious layer of cream. The
cake is left to dry out slightly before being thoroughly soaked in the
milks and spread with a final layer of cream. It may be simply served
in the traditional Mexican way, with a dusting of cinnamon, or it can
be dressed up with garnishes of fresh fruit, nuts, caramel, chocolate,
coconut or liqueurs. The cake became widespread across Latin
America during the 1940s, when Nestlé began to print the recipe on
cans of evaporated milk and condensed milk. It travelled to North
America with Latinx immigrants nostalgic for the recipes of their
childhood, and has since been taken to heart across the country. The
tres leches cake has a reputation as a great party cake, standing
testament to the pleasures offered by sweet simplicity.

The tres leches cake has rather a reputation as a ladies' cake:
it is a very popular choice for afternoon teas, *quinceañeras*
(a Mexican coming-of-age party for fifteen-year-old girls)
and engagement parties.

Trifle

The trifle transcends its own name and is anything
but a small and insignificant dessert.

• • • • •

This is Britain's no-holds-barred take on the 'plain cake soaked with
booze and garnished with cream' model — lovingly assembled to a
cherished formula, according to family tradition. Individual variations
fluctuate from one grandmother's recipe to the next, but all trifles
unanimously include sponge sprinkled with alcohol, egg custard, fruit
and whipped cream, and are ideally made in a high-sided glass dish
to show off the pretty layers. The sponge layer could be jam rolls or
sponge fingers, the custard fresh or boxed and the liquor port, sherry
or Cointreau. Fruit options include peaches, apricots or berries,
either fresh or from a can. This is a special-occasion dessert and is
garnished accordingly, often with cubes of red jelly, glacé cherries,
slivered almonds, raspberry sauce, toffee and yet more fruit.

Upside Down Cake

Just as it sounds, this cake is baked with a layer
of caramelised fruit at the base and then inverted
for serving, to display the fruit on top.

• • • • •

Following in the footsteps of cobblers and other desserts that marry
fruit with a simple cake base, this particular variety of cake was born
in the USA in the late 1800s. Not only did it look attractive, it was also
easily prepared — bakers without an oven could easily make it in a
skillet on the stove. The most notorious of the upside down cakes is
the classic version made with tinned pineapple rings and maraschino
cherries; when the cake is inverted after baking, a garish yellow-
and-red arrangement of fruit is revealed. In the 1920s, both these
ingredients represented the height of exotic chic: the cherries were
imported from Europe, and the pineapple stormed America as the
result of a highly successful promotional campaign by the Hawaiian
Pineapple Company. These days, sightings are relatively rare, and
almost exclusively as the star attraction of retro-themed dinner parties.

A French application of much the same technique produced
the famous *tarte Tatin*, named after two sisters who ran an inn south
of Paris and first served the dish. Apples are cooked in a buttery
caramel, then covered with puff pastry, baked and served with cream
or ice cream. It remains one of France's most-loved desserts.

Vínaterta

Nicknamed the 'striped lady' *(randalín)* for its
many fine layers, this cake stands proud as a symbol
of Iceland's culinary identity.

• • • • •

The *vínaterta* is built with up to nine alternating storeys of almond
shortbread and fruit compote spiced with cardamom, vanilla or
red wine. Often rectangular in shape, it is iced with a simple sugar
glaze flavoured with vodka or bourbon. Although *vínaterta* translates
as 'Viennese cake', the Icelandic version was merely inspired by the
layered cakes of Austria, incorporating local rhubarb in the filling
as one notable point of difference. Despite being a rather simple
cake, it is nonetheless treasured as a significant symbol of Icelandic
cuisine by expatriate communities in Canada and America. Many of
their ancestors were forced to relocate in the late 1800s, when a
volcanic explosion decimated the farming and fishing industries, and
the *vínaterta* has become a powerful reminder of their homeland.

Homespun
Recipes

. . . . .

I am not a professional baker by any stretch of the imagination, so I prefer to stick to the simpler formulae for making cakes, i.e. not too many ingredients and certainly not too many complicated procedures. What follows are a few cakes I always return to. They're not overly complex to make but allow plenty of room for creativity, as even basic cakes can provide a platform for handsome decoration.

ALL OF THESE RECIPES WILL SERVE ROUGHLY 8–10

Carrot Cake

· · · · ·

Due to the inclusion of a salad ingredient, the carrot cake has a reputation as a healthy option — a misapprehension I am more than happy to embrace. The natural sweetness of the carrots combined with the crunchy walnuts, mild spicing and sweet raisins create a wonderfully textured cake, balanced deliciously by its thick crown of tangy cream cheese icing. The way it brings together sweet, sour, spicy and savoury flavours makes this one of my favourite cakes. If you wish to make it for a special occasion, double the recipe and layer two of the cakes with more cream-cheese icing between them.

INGREDIENTS

For the cake

125 g carrot, grated
(about 5 carrots)

275 g brown sugar

160 ml vegetable oil

3 eggs

210 g plain flour

1½ tsp bicarbonate soda

1 tsp ground cinnamon

½ tsp ground ginger

45 g walnuts, chopped,
plus whole walnuts to garnish

75 g sultanas

For the icing

250 g cream cheese

55 g icing sugar

1½ Tbsp lemon juice

1 Tbsp lemon zest

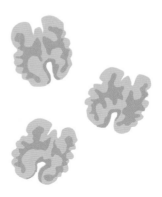

METHOD

Preheat the oven to 180°C. Grease a 22 cm round cake tin using butter or oil and line the base with baking paper.

Start off by peeling then finely grating the carrots, then set them aside.

In a large bowl, add the sugar and the oil and beat for a few minutes until pale and frothy, then gradually add in the eggs and continue to beat until they are completely incorporated.

Sieve all the cake's dry ingredients into the bowl with the wet ingredients and mix.

Add the grated carrot, walnuts and sultanas, and fold gently until just combined.

Pour the mixture into your cake tin and cook for approximately 1 hour. Cool the cake in the tin.

To make the icing, beat the cream cheese with the icing sugar, lemon juice and zest in a food processor, or by hand, until smooth.

Once the cake has cooled, spread the icing over the cake and decorate with a ring of whole walnuts.

See page 35

Chocolate Cake

· · · · ·

For me, the pinnacle of deliciousness is usually something chocolate flavoured. Chocolate with nuts, with orange, with coffee, with rum, with mint — all delicious. This chocolate cake gets its richness from the almond meal used in place of flour, and the olive oil used in place of butter adds another dimension of flavour. The ganache topping elevates the whole thing from an everyday cake to a special dessert cake and provides the opportunity to add further flavour profiles to the cake. You can follow the chocaholic path of a pure chocolate ganache, or try adding some orange zest, coffee, or rum to the basic recipe.

METHOD

Preheat the oven to 170°C. Grease a 22 cm round cake tin using butter or oil and line the base with baking paper.

In a small bowl, whisk the cocoa powder into the boiling water to form a smooth paste. Swirl in the vanilla extract and set aside.

In another small bowl, combine the ground almonds with the bicarb soda and a pinch of salt.

In a third, larger bowl, combine the sugar with the olive oil and eggs and beat vigorously for 3–5 minutes until pale and frothy. Continue to beat whilst gradually incorporating the cocoa mixture, then add in the dry ingredients and stir to combine.

Pour the mix into your tin and bake for 40–45 minutes. Allow the cake to cool in the tin for 10 minutes before removing it and transferring to a rack.

To make the ganache, start by setting up a double boiler (or bain-marie). To do this, place a glass or metal bowl over a pot of boiling water on the stove, ensuring that the bottom of the bowl doesn't touch the boiling water below.

Roughly chop the chocolate and add it to the bowl, stirring regularly. Once it's melted, add the cream and continue to stir until the mix is almost boiling. Add your flavouring of choice, if any, then put the bowl in the fridge to cool for at least 30 minutes.

Once cooled, beat the mixture vigorously until aerated and smooth. Spread the ganache over the cake and decorate with berries, nuts or grated chocolate.

The basic cake recipe for this is based on Nigella Lawson's 'Chocolate Olive Oil Cake' from *Nigellissima*, but the ganache is my own.

INGREDIENTS

For the cake

50 g best quality cocoa powder
125 ml water, boiling
2 tsp vanilla extract
150 g ground almonds
½ tsp bicarbonate soda
1 pinch salt
200 g caster sugar
150 ml olive oil
3 eggs

For the ganache

200 g very dark chocolate
250 ml heavy cream

OPTIONAL EXTRAS

1 Tbsp rum or Cointreau
1–½ Tbsp orange zest
1 Tbsp fresh orange juice
1 Tbsp espresso

Lemon Tart

· · · · ·

This is a favourite in my family, and once you get your head around making pastry the rest is extremely easy. I'm a big enthusiast of sweet and sour flavours, and this is always a luscious and refreshing end to a meal. I use an unsweetened pastry case because I like the savoury flavour of the tart shell without sugar, but feel free to substitute with a sweet pastry recipe if you prefer. The filling of the tart calls for half lemon juice, half orange — but you can use whatever citrus you have on hand (a bit of lime will be fine, for example). The orange is there to offset the sour lemon, but if you think you can handle it go ahead and replace it with more lemon juice. The tart is best served with cream, to soften the sourness.

INGREDIENTS

For the pastry
240 g plain flour
1 pinch salt
180 g butter, chilled
60 ml water, iced

For the filling
4 eggs
200 g caster sugar
1 Tbsp lemon zest
120 ml lemon juice
120 ml orange juice
2 tsp pouring cream

To serve
Heavy cream
Finely sliced lemon wedges
or lemon zest

METHOD

Grease a 24 cm fluted tart tin using butter or oil, and line the base with baking paper.

For the pastry, mix the flour and salt in a large bowl, then grate in the butter using a hand grater. Rub this mixture between your fingers until it forms a crumb-like texture, then slowly add in the water and form into a ball. Do not over mix.

Refrigerate the pastry for 30 minutes, preheating the oven to 180°C while you wait.

Once chilled, remove the pastry and roll it out on a floured surface so that it's about 3–5 mm thick.

Gently lay the sheet of pastry over your prepared tin and press it in, trimming off any excess (chef's treat!) using a sharp knife. Blind bake the shell for 15 minutes, using rice or cooking weights to prevent it puffing up. After 15 minutes, remove the rice/weights and allow the case to colour for a further few minutes before removing from the oven and allowing to cool slightly.

For the filling, beat the eggs with the sugar, zest and pouring cream until light and frothy. Add the citrus juices and mix to combine.

Carefully pour the mixture into the shell and bake until the centre is just set (but not yet firm). This should take about 20 minutes, but you can wobble the tart a bit to test if it's done.

Decorate the tart with finely sliced lemon wedges (candied in a pan with sugar, if you like) or a sprinkling of lemon zest.

Serve cold, with cream.

See page 64

Pavlova

·····

A classic in Australia, and often exactly the right thing to finish a meal during the heat of summer festivities. It's simple enough to make, so long as you don't adopt too casual an attitude to the separation of the eggs (I've learned this the hard way). The perfect bake is also a matter of taste, as some prefer a soft centre whilst others like it dried to a crisp — it's an art you'll just have to bake a few pavlovas to refine. The 'pav' can be garnished with any fruit that takes your fancy — some of my favourites are, variously, strawberries, raspberries, blueberries, blackberries, passionfuit, mango, kiwi, peaches, nectarines and apricots. Or you can forego the fruit and crumble over chocolate, ground coffee and chopped nuts instead. Liqueur in the cream is a delicious and highly recommended grown-up twist, too.

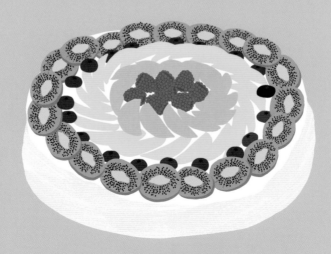

METHOD

Preheat your oven to 180°C. Wipe a large bowl with a cut lemon before you begin, to remove any trace of fat.

Separate the egg yolks and whites, adding the whites to the cleaned bowl. Take care that not even the tiniest bit of yolk gets in with the whites, or you will end up with a flat pav, (which can be rescued by rolling with cream and berries to become a roulade). You can discard the yolks or use them for something else (like the Tiramisu on page 125, for example).

Beat the egg whites until foamy, then add cream of tartar and continue to beat until you have a thick, glossy mixture. Then, add the sugar, cornflour, vinegar and vanilla extract and beat vigorously until the mixture forms very stiff peaks.

Arrange some baking paper on an oven tray and spread your meringue mixture in a circle in the centre, so that it's about 5 cm thick.

Place into the hot oven and turn down the temperature to 150°C. Cook for 1 hour and 25 minutes, then turn off the oven and allow the pavlova to completely cool inside — this will help minimise cracking. If you're a fan of a chewy centre, reduce the cooking time to about 50 minutes.

When ready to serve, whip the cream with the vanilla (and liqueur, if using) until thick, then spread over the cooled meringue and top with an artful arrangement of your desired fruit.

You can also make these pavlovas in miniature for individual serves. Just split the mixture into 8–10 smaller circles on the baking paper and reduce the cooking time to 30 minutes.

See page 78

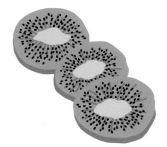

INGREDIENTS

For the base

4 eggs, whites only
(at room temperature)

¼ tsp cream of tartar

200 g caster sugar

1 tsp cornflour

1 tsp white vinegar

1 tsp vanilla extract

For the garnish

400 ml whipping cream
(approx.)

1 tsp vanilla extract

Fruit of choice, chopped

Sponge Cake

· · · · ·

The light and airy base that is a friend to so many of the world's favourite cakes. This is my grandmother's recipe and was the show-stopping birthday cake through childhood that always impressed us. She would sandwich the sponges with cream and strawberries between them, glazing the top with a pink-coloured lemon icing decorated with coloured sprinkles, tiny silver balls and, usually, birthday candles. This is basically what I've specified here, but the sponge is a blank canvas so experiment with the filling, icing and garnishes as you feel.

INGREDIENTS

For the cake

4 eggs

150 g caster sugar

95 g cornflour

1 Tbsp custard powder

½ tsp bicarbonate soda

1 tsp cream of tartar

1 pinch of salt

For the filling

240 ml whipping cream

1 tsp icing sugar

½ tsp vanilla extract

1 (250 g) punnet strawberries
or other berries

For the icing

160 g icing sugar

2 Tbsp lemon juice

A few drops of red
food colouring

METHOD

Preheat your oven to 190°C. Grease two 20 cm cake tins using butter or oil and line the base with baking paper.

Separate the eggs, placing the whites in a large bowl and the yolks in a smaller, separate bowl to the side. Whip the egg whites to form medium peaks, then continue to whip as you slowly add the caster sugar. Once all the sugar is incorporated, slowly add in the yolks as you beat the mixture well.

In a separate bowl, sieve the cake's dry ingredients (twice), then slowly add them to your egg mixture, folding as you go. Do not over mix!

Divide the mixture equally between the two tins and bake for exactly 20 minutes — or until golden brown and springy to touch. Allow the cakes to cool in the tins for 10 minutes, then remove and allow to cool completely on a rack before filling or icing.

To make the filling, add the icing sugar and vanilla extract to the cream, whip into stiff peaks and set aside.

To make the icing, pour the icing sugar into a bowl and gradually stir in the lemon juice until you have a thick, slightly runny consistency — you may need to add a little water. Stir in the food colouring.

Finely slice the strawberries if using. To assemble, spread the cream over the first cake and layer up with your chosen berries. Add the second cake and glaze the top with the icing. Finish with sprinkles or more berries.

See page 97

Tiramisu

· · · · ·

Pudding-like desserts are my preferred type, and the combination of coffee and cream is a long-time favourite. I like my tiramisu quite wet — like a trifle — and very heavy on the coffee and boozy flavours. This dessert can be assembled to your desired consistency, and the flavours can easily be adjusted to taste. I love Marsala wine in my tiramisu, but Cointreau or Frangelico liqueurs can be substituted. Grated orange zest in the cream is nice, and dark chocolate shavings between each layer are also a welcome addition.

METHOD

My mum always uses a deep 22 x 23 cm rectangular dish for this, but I prefer a large bowl; so go with whatever suits you.

In a large mixing bowl, beat the heavy cream with one tablespoon of the sugar until it forms stiff peaks.

In another bowl, whisk the egg yolks with the remaining sugar until creamy, then slowly incorporate the mascarpone.

Add in the whipped cream and slowly mix until smooth. If you wish to add any orange zest to the cream, now's the time.

Mix together the coffee and Marsala in a separate bowl. Briefly dip each biscuit in the coffee mixture, then arrange to cover the bottom of your chosen dish.

Spread a layer of the cream mixture over the biscuits (add chocolate shavings here, if using), then start again with another layer of biscuits, then another layer of cream, etc. The number of layers will depend on the size of your dish — but make sure you end up topping it with a layer of cream!

To finish, dust with a fine layer of cocoa powder.

See page 103

INGREDIENTS

180 ml whipping cream

5 Tbsp sugar

4 eggs, yolks only

500 g mascarpone

500 ml espresso

6 Tbsp Marsala wine or liqueur of choice

24 Savoiardi (ladyfinger) biscuits

Cocoa powder, to serve

Acknowledgements

· · · · ·

As my life becomes more serious (and my palate increasingly savoury), I've come to appreciate more than ever the pure fun offered up by a visit to the cake shop. This slightly mad book came about as testament to the power of cakes – their luxurious flavours, outrageous decoration and extraordinary command over our emotions.

To Kirsten Abbott, I must extend an enormous thank you for indulging my love of cakes – especially the green ones and the cultural curiosity on pages 94–5. Who better to understand the feeling I get when I admire baked goods than she who had a giant *pièce montée* of pink-iced choux puffs wrapped in ribbons and roses for her wedding cake? It's good to know I'm not alone.

To Ashlea O'Neill, another huge thank you for designing the book. Collaboration is what I love most about my job, and your elegant and playful style brilliantly shows off all the cakes at their best – we'd just have a scrapbook without you.

To my editors, Sam Palfreyman and Alison Cowan – I'm so glad you also share an enthusiasm for cake, as I made you both read and re-read my thoughts on it again and again. Special mentions go to Sam, a better baker than I, for helping me to properly articulate my nuanced feelings about cake; and to Alison, whose wisdom and advice on such important subjects as 'to choux or not to choux?' were greatly appreciated.

To Caitlin O'Reardon and all the team at Thames & Hudson Australia, my most heartfelt thanks for the opportunity to write my first book – and on the subject of a lifelong passion, no less.

I'd also like to acknowledge three heavy reference books, which extended my cake knowledge beyond my own personal experience – *The Oxford Companion to Food* by Alan Davidson (OUP, 1999/2014), *The Oxford Companion to Sugar and Sweets* edited by Darra Goldstein (OUP, 2015) and the venerable *Larousse Gastronomique* by Prosper Montagné (Hamlyn Publishing Group, 1938/1988).

Finally, to my parents, who are responsible for taking me to the patisserie from a young age: thank you for allowing me many a 'special treat' over the years – but just the good stuff, no junk. Though you have taught me to maintain a balanced diet, it is, unfortunately, still punctuated with frequent acts of rebellion. Further thanks go to the women in my family – particularly my mum, sister and grandmother – who have always baked brilliantly for me, while I can really only eat brilliantly in return.

Biography

· · · · ·

Alice Oehr is an artist and designer from Melbourne, Australia. Her dynamic illustrations have been featured in print and across products, parties, packaging and textiles. She honed her eye for cakes over a lifetime of visits to France – where the local patisserie provided many a bribe for a fussy-eating child – and these days still enjoys a cake, though mostly of the more grown-up boozy or bittersweet variety. Alice believes cake decoration is a high art and has a special fondness for cakes covered in green marzipan and cherries.

First published in 2020 in the United States of America by
Thames & Hudson Inc., 500 Fifth Avenue, New York, New York 10110

www.thamesandhudsonusa.com

The Art of Cake © 2020 Thames & Hudson Australia
Text and illustrations © 2020 Alice Oehr

ISBN 978-1-760-76075-5

Library of Congress Control Number: 2019954499

Design: Ashlea O'Neill
Editing: Alison Cowan
Printed and bound in China by RR Donnelley

FSC® is dedicated to the promotion of responsible forest management worldwide.
This book is made of material from FSC®-certified forests and other controlled sources.

MIX
Paper from
responsible sources
FSC® C144853
FSC
www.fsc.org